D1502391

TANKS

Valerie Bodden

CREATIVE ✦ EDUCATION

Published by Creative Education
P.O. Box 227, Mankato, Minnesota 56002
Creative Education is an imprint of The Creative Company
www.thecreativecompany.us

Design and production by Liddy Walseth
Art direction by Rita Marshall
Printed by Corporate Graphics in the United States of America

Photographs by Alamy (Reelexposures), Getty Images (Don Farrall, David Higgs, Purestock,
Stocktrek, Stocktrek Images), iStockphoto (Akiyoko, Barnaby Chambers, Jared DeCinque,
Gary Blakeley, Rich Koele, Narvikk), Shutterstock (ID 1974, Zastol skiy Victor Leonidovich, Ran Z)

Library of Congress Cataloging-in-Publication Data

Bodden, Valerie.
Tanks / by Valerie Bodden.
p. cm. — (Built for battle)
Summary: A fundamental exploration of tanks, including their size and firepower, history of development,
crawler tracks and other features, and famous models from around the world.
Includes bibliographical references and index.
ISBN 978-1-60818-129-2
1. Tanks (Military science)—Juvenile literature. I. Title. II. Series.
UG446.5.B595 2012
623.7′4752—dc22 2010054406

CPSIA: 030111 PO1447

First edition
2 4 6 8 9 7 5 3 1

TANKS

Valerie Bodden

TABLE OF
contents

5. What Is a Tank?

9. Early Tanks

11. Sizes and Parts

14. Tank Tracks

19. Tank Crews

20. Tanks in Battle

FAMOUS TANKS

8. T-34

16. Chieftain Mk 5

23. M1 Abrams

24. Glossary

24. Index

24. Web Sites

24. Read More

A low rumbling sound fills the air.

It gets closer and louder. Suddenly, a long

line of huge vehicles roars past.

These are tanks!

Tanks are vehicles that have ARMOR and move on tracks. They have big guns to shoot at enemy vehicles, buildings, and soldiers. Tanks today move across the ground at 30 to 50 miles (48-80 km) per hour.

A tank from Russia climbing up and over a mound of dirt

★ **Famous Tank** ★

T-34

COUNTRY

Soviet Union

ENTERED SERVICE

1940

LENGTH

20 feet (6.1 m)

WIDTH

9.8 feet (3 m)

WEIGHT

30.9 tons (28 t)

FASTEST SPEED

25 miles (40 km) per hour

CREW

4

Thousands of T-34s were built between 1940 and 1958. It was the second-most-built tank of all time. T-34 tanks were used by 40 different countries!

The first tanks were built during WORLD WAR I. They moved slowly. Later, bigger, faster tanks with powerful guns were built.

A side view of a tank
from the United States
firing its big gun

Today, the biggest tanks weigh 70 tons (63.5 t). That is as much as eight elephants! Most tanks are about 20 to 30 feet (6.1-9.1 m) long and about 10 feet (3 m) wide.

The box-shaped bottom part of a tank is called the hull. The TURRET sits on top of the hull. The tank's big, main gun is attached to the turret. The turret spins to point the gun in any direction.

A tank moves on tracks, or treads. The tracks are long metal and rubber belts that loop over wheels on each side of the tank. The tracks help the tank move over rough ground. They can move tanks through shallow water!

A close-up view of the tracks going around a tank's wheels

Chieftain Mk 5

☆ **Famous Tank** ☆

COUNTRY

Great Britain

ENTERED SERVICE

1966

LENGTH

24.7 feet (7.5 m)

WIDTH

11.5 feet (3.5 m)

WEIGHT

54 tons (49 t)

FASTEST SPEED

30 miles (48 km) per hour

CREW

4

The Chieftain had heavier armor
and a more powerful main gun
than any other tank when it was built.
Its low hull meant that the driver
had to lie back to steer.

Most tanks have three or four crew members. The driver sits or lies back in the hull to steer the tank. The other crew members sit in the turret. The commander gives orders. The gunner fires the main gun. In some tanks, a loader puts SHELLS in the gun. It can get very hot inside the tank.

When a tank goes into battle, the crew closes its hatches, or openings. They use PERISCOPES to see outside. The gunner uses a computer to help him aim the tank's big gun. Then he fires it. The crew might fire smaller guns, too.

A crew member coming out of a tank's hatch by a machine gun

Tanks usually travel in groups. They protect each other and other vehicles and soldiers. A tank's armor protects it from enemy bullets, GRENADES (*gruh-NAYDZ*), and other weapons. It keeps the tank safe to fight another day!

M1 Abrams

COUNTRY

United States

ENTERED SERVICE

1983

LENGTH

32.3 feet (9.8 m)

WIDTH

12 feet (3.7 m)

WEIGHT

56 tons (51 t)

FASTEST SPEED

42 miles (68 km) per hour

CREW

4

The Abrams tank has one of the most powerful main guns of any tank in the world today. It can fire shells at targets more than two miles (3.2 km) away!

GLOSSARY

armor—a layer of metal and other strong materials that covers a military vehicle and protects it from attacks

grenades—small bombs that soldiers can throw with their hands or shoot from guns

periscopes—sets of tubes and mirrors used to give a view of what is happening outside; in a tank, the periscopes look like small, rectangular windows

shells—objects that are shot from a large gun and are filled with materials that can explode

turret—part of a tank that has guns attached to it and can turn to point in different directions

World War I—a war from 1914 to 1918 in which Great Britain, France, Russia, the U.S., and other countries fought against Germany, Turkey, and other countries

INDEX

armor 6, 16, 22

Chieftain Mk 5 16

crews 8, 16, 19, 20, 23

guns 6, 9, 12, 16, 19, 20, 23

hulls 12, 16, 19

M1 Abrams 23

periscopes 20

size 8, 11, 16, 23

speed 6, 8, 16, 23

T-34 8

tracks 6, 14

turrets 12, 19

World War I 9

WEB SITES

Super Coloring: Military Coloring Pages

http://www.supercoloring.com/pages/category/military/
Print and color pictures of all your favorite military machines.

U.S. Army Info Site: Abrams Main Battle Tank

http://www.us-army-info.com/pages/pics/abrams.html
Check out pictures of Abrams tanks in action.

READ MORE

David, Jack. *Abrams Tanks.* Minneapolis: Torque Books, 2008.

Demarest, Chris. *Alpha, Bravo, Charlie: The Military Alphabet.* New York: Margaret K. McElderry Books, 2005.